Praise for *We Are Not Mahogany*:

"Stories of the lives of African men that are bound to strike you at the heart."

"Excellent resource for learning and discourse."

"A profound read. Instant meaning."

"It is like opening a little window into life half a world away."

We Are Not Mahogany

Three stories about the
male African life.

We Are Not Mahogany

Mahogany

by
Dr. Nathaniel Dunigan

Life Metrics Media

ISBN: 978-1499337655

To my participants, with respect and gratitude.

We Are Not Mahogany

TABLE OF CONTENTS

THURSDAY   1

LUKE   15

BENNETT   27

QUESTIONS FOR DISCUSSION AND
REFLECTION   37

FURTHER DISCUSSION   41

ACKNOWLEDGEMENTS   59

UGANDA   55

BIBLIOGRAPHY   58

ABOUT THE AUTHOR   61

Foreword

These short stories are taken directly from the findings section of my doctoral dissertation. In my research, I explored the ways that Ugandan men perceive manhood, and how that influences their choices in life. I used a fictional narrative to report what I learned.

In this narrative, three characters tell us their life stories. First, a man named Thursday tell us his. He is a composite character of my participants aged 27, 28 and 37. Next we hear from Luke who represents the men aged 45, 48 and 54. In a country with an average male life expectancy of 54.5 years, Luke is among the oldest living men in Uganda. Finally, Bennett shares his story and his outlook on the future. He represents men aged 18, 19, and 20 who are currently students in Secondary School (akin to American High School).

I chose to present these stories out of chronological order because I wanted to start with Thursday. He has more engagement with the other two characters so he is able to introduce us to them. And I end with Bennett, the youngest character, because he has more of an unwritten story ahead of him, a compelling notion in this exploration of the construction of masculinity and the implications for the future.

In my opening remarks at my dissertation proposal defense I said, "I want to be careful to be mindful of that fact that I am proposing a study that is going to ask men to share with me their lived experiences, the most joyous and most horrific parts of their lives, and I always want to be careful to honor that, including here at the beginning." It is my sincerest desire that these short stories be seen through that lens. As often as I could, I used the participants' own words to tell these stories. (All words in italics are taken directly from the transcripts.) This compromised my normal writing style, but hopefully elevated the notion of authenticity--and honor. The men remain in my thoughts and prayers daily.

Nathaniel Dunigan, PhD, EdM
San Diego

We Are Not Mahogany

From the pages of the dissertation entitled

We Are Not Mahogany: An exploration of the social construction of masculinity in Ugandan meaning-making

For more information, visit
www.DrDunigan.com.

Notes for the Reader

The italicized words come directly from the interview transcripts.

At the end of this text, Dr. Dunigan has included some discussion questions and further analysis to highlight how the stories demonstrated his dissertation findings. These might be used for book club discussions or for personal reflection.

Thursday

My name is Thursday. They call me that because I was born on a Thursday. *I hate my name.*

The year is 2001, and I am 15 years old. I grew up in a classroom. My mother was very young when I was born. Until I was old enough to go to school on my own, everyday she would use a kitenge to tie me onto her back, and carry me to school. There, she would lay out the kitenge on the cement floor in one corner of the crowded room where her mom, my grandmom, was a primary school teacher. I still remember playing in that corner, and the feeling of being wrapped up on her back as she made the long walk home on the red dirt streets of Kampala. Motorcycle taxis, called boda-bodas, zipped past us on all sides, hooting at us with their squeaky little horns, while giant Maribou Storks lumbered around us, picking at the garbage piles that lined the streets. When we would get home, Mom would either give me sugarcane to chew on or a cup of milk chai to drink, depending on whether it was the hot, dry season, or the cold, rainy season.

When I completed Primary 7 at school, my grandmom also retired from teaching. This meant that there was no money for school fees, so I have had to sit at home since.

I don't know who my father is, and that disturbs me a lot. When I ask about him, I am ignored. This means I don't know which clan I belong to or anything about my lineage. This is a problem. It also means that I don't know which clan I cannot marry into, and I don't know where I will be buried. You see, I am meant to be laid to rest with my father's family, but I don't know where their graves are. Many times my friends have *found me seated and keeping quiet. When they ask me what's wrong, I reply, "I am having my own problems," like that. But these days they are used to me because whenever they find me like that, my grandmom calls me and tells me, "No, don't think of that," and she tries to encourage me.*

There are many people in our small house today. I don't know exactly how many. The house is made up of seven rooms, and as always, every door is closed. We received a visitor two days ago; a woman a bit older than Mom. They told me that she used to work here as a housemaid.

When you first enter our house, you find a room lined with furniture. To the left of the door is a large, stuffed armchair covered in maroon and gold fabric with gold tassels dangling from each arm. Next to it is a sofa with bright blue and green stripes. This one is my favorite because it extends to the corner and is under the window. When I can't fall sleep on the mattress that I normally share with my cousin, I come to this sofa, and it always makes me sleepy. There is another sofa just like it on the opposite wall, but there are doors on each side of it, one leading to the kitchen, and the other to the bathroom. I hate sitting there, let alone sleeping there.

Along the wall that connects the two sofa-walls are two more maroon and gold chairs, one on each side of the door that leads to the hallway. We have only a few things hanging on our walls. One is a photo of Oprah Winfrey. My sister cut it out of the newspaper. There are also our baptism certificates from church, a photo of Pope John Paul II, and a photo of President Museveni. (They were giving these photos out at school before I had to stop going.)

Off of the hallway are four rooms that we use for bedrooms. Grandmom's room is the last one. I have only been in her room once in my lifetime.

In the kitchen, cooking is done on a charcoal stove on the floor. We do our washing outside, by hand. I wash my clothes and my mom's, except for her underclothes. In Uganda, everyone washes their own underwear. I am told that even President Museveni washes his own shorts!

Dinner tonight was my favorite: rice, beans and avocado. I am not sure who prepared it, but they used enough garlic and salt to make it perfect.

We were gathered in the sitting room after dinner when my grandmom suddenly said, "That one is your real mom," she used her lips to point to the former housemaid, our visitor.

"What? What do you mean?" I ask.

"After she stopped working for us, she went somewhere and got pregnant. After you were born, she brought you here saying she couldn't manage you, so we decided to be Good Samaritans and take you up."

Nothing further is said to me. And I don't know what to say or do.

One of my uncles switches on the radio. It's 11pm. Everyone begins to listen as the announcer reads personal notices, hoping to hear messages from family upcountry. People often go to their local office of the national radio station, and pay a few hundred shillings to send greetings or death announcements to family in other parts of the country.

I find myself staring at the former housemaid. "She's not my mom," I think to myself. "She can't be. Why is my grandmom trying to deceive me?"

I get up and go outside. It's very dark. The electricity has just gone out again. This is the fifth or sixth time today. I have lost count. Street vendors at the corner are lighting candles to illuminate their wares: matchboxes, batteries, candles, tiny bars of soap, salt, and flip-flop shower shoes.

I hear a baby crying next door, and in the distance, the sounds of lorries beginning their late night trek across eastern Uganda to collect imported items at the Kenyan border. Items that originated in Europe and India, then shipped across the Indian Ocean to Mombasa, and then through the entire expanse of Kenya before finally reaching Uganda. Some of the items will remain here, while others will be taken to the Congolese border to the west.

I make my own journey down our dark street, and call out for my friend in the direction of his house. No response. I call out several more times. Finally, he opens his front door, and comes to greet me.

"Yes, Thursday! Ki kati? What's up?"

"Don't call me that. You know I hate my name," I say.

He then calls me "Baambi," a term of endearment in Luganda. He says he's sorry, and then adds, "Ki ki gwe? What's wrong with you? Are you again thinking about your father?"

"Worse," I say. "Can you imagine? They have just informed me that the other woman is my mom."

"Who told you? Which woman do you mean? Be clear," he demands. And I explain. He takes my left arm by wrapping his right hand around my wrist, and he pulls me to the broken stoop in front of his house. We sit. The uneven concrete has captured some of that afternoon's rain, but I don't care.

"I feared telling you such," he says.

"You mean you KNEW?"

He raises and drops his eyebrows in one dramatic movement. This means yes.

"It's not true," I say. "I won't believe it. I refuse."

"There's more," he swallows. He's no longer looking at me. "She was impregnated by one of the men in your house while she was a housemaid there. I don't know which man, but that's why they have raised you. One of them is your father, and the one you call Mom is your sister."

I shook his hand free from my wrist and walked away, but I didn't go home. "None of this is true. People are just lying, the usual sadists trying to cause damage," I tell myself. I wait outside until my house has gone quiet before I reenter. Once inside, I lay down on the blue and green sofa, but tonight I fail to catch sleep. They expect me to believe that behind one of these closed doors is a stranger who is my mother, and an uncle who is my dad.

But I do not.

~

Two weeks pass, and nothing more is said.

Then, grandmum announces that the whole family will gather at the house. They are going to give me a new name and decide which clan will be mine.

When the day finally came, I was so excited. When I first arrived, I found all my uncles and aunts taking Nile Special beers. They like to drink them through a straw, and at room temperature, right out of the bottles. The kids were taking sodas in the same way. These beverages always mean that a good time is in store.

At first, all the aunts and uncles said I should be a member of the Nkima (meaning vervet monkey) clan. But my grandmom said no. She wanted me to have her same clan, the Mmamba (meaning lungfish) clan. After much discussion, at last they agreed that their mum, my grandmum, should decide. So now I am of the Mmamba clan, and my name is Mukasa Patrick. On Sunday I am to be baptized with these names at the Catholic church where we attend every Sunday.

While I am happier with this identity, I still often wonder where my real dad is, and what my actual identity is. Anyway, they have tried their level best to help me so that I can grow up, and move through a proper Ugandan life.

Still, I am so short. The kids around me often say, "You ka-small boy, you come." Yesterday, they laughed at me when I tried to compete in a running race. *Being short, I didn't manage to beat the other guys because they are too fast!*

After five years of sitting at home, my Kojja Luke, a lay priest and a teacher came to visit. Together with Grandmom, we talked about school and how badly I wished to study. *I asked them if I should go with him to his parish, VERY deep in the village, where he was working as the school's chaplain.* I went.

But I jumped the classes there. From Form 2, I just went direct to Form 4, and at the end of the year, I didn't score well. I know it's because I was missing Form 3, but he didn't want me to repeat. He told me to look for yet another school where I could continue even with my low grades.

I found one, but I couldn't afford the boarding fees. But one of my uncle's friends, *a Reverend Father, had a deaf school and he had a lot of simple rooms which were not being used, so I asked him whether I could stay there and help him in some work. And the Father accepted because he knew me. He was* my uncle's *parish priest. They are still friends.*

So I stayed at the deaf school, and *I was feeding on the school meals, but the father would allocate us a lot of work, including escorting the students to the well to fetch water; we could move on the trucks to go and bring firewood; we could move on the trucks to the villages to buy beans.* There were several of us living and eating there, and we were the ones who did all of this work. *And I could not get enough time* to study.

I did not tell my uncle because I feared. They are all priests. Instead I struggled, I strived very much to see that at least I preserve time to study, *but I couldn't. Because the moment you don't do the work they have told you* to do, *they come and they tell him, and that was something very bad. They could quarrel, and he could see us as useless people, so we could try our level best to do what he wanted us to do.*

Sometimes you could miss some days of school because you had to go to village to bring the beans for the school. You could miss a lot of things at school. So A-level, my Senior Six, I did not pass very well. I scored just one principle pass, and the others were subsidiaries. But I did not tell him why I passed poorly, so he told me, "You look for yourself a vocational school."

I came to Kampala. I came back to my grandmom's place and I started looking for a school at Kampala. And I found one. *They give me Hotel Management and Institutional Catering, a two-year diploma course.*

When I started, I learned that they were in the middle of campaigns for student government. *I joined the campaign as a candidate for the Guild President's position, and I won! I won the election!* This meant that I did not have to pay tuition or any of the fees. *So my uncle remained with buying for me just personal requirements.*

For two years, I was the Guild President. I served until when I was finishing my studies. That is when I handed over. God helped me very much, and my uncle and my grandmom struggled for my life. I now help the son to my cousin-brother in the same way. He's called Bennett. (I call him "Big Boy Bennett" because he's not short like me.) He actually sat at home for two years before I came to realize that he did not have fees for school. He's had some rough times lately, but he is a wise kid with good marks and a positive outlook.

Shortly after I earned my diploma, my uncle had a stroke. He lost everything a man does in life to look after his family members. From that time, I started to look after my family, my sisters, taking them to school, helping to buy food and pay rents. I call those *my sad days.*

But now I have my own son, and I am so happy. His name is Henry. He is one-and-a-half years old, but he behaves *like someone of four years.* He is *really, really, really a good boy.* When I get home from work, *he pulls off the socks from my legs, takes them where the dirty clothes are. Knowing that when Daddy comes home he has to take a shower, he brings the things to go and bathe, like a towel.*

He knows where the drinks are. He can go and get the cup, go in the fridge. Though he is short, he can pull out the jerry-can for the water. He knows where the books are, the pen. When his mom is sitting down, he can go and bring the book and the pen, sit there, trying to write at that age!

I also have a good woman now. I am so lucky. *Most women don't know what they really want. Like 70% of them are not patient. God gave them to us to help us, but they have not done their work at home. Maybe God is annoyed by that.* But my woman is good. *I wear a ring* on my left ring-finger even though we are not yet married. But *my heart is married.* One day, I shall have enough money to pay for all the traditional ceremonies to make it official. I have plans to open a business where my sisters can work and earn their own money, and then maybe also help me, too.

God has given me creativity in my head. I thank God for that. I also have what I call *the blood of leadership. Most people don't have that. Leadership is a gift given or provided by God to some people. That is why you find sometimes, people when they are given opportunities, they just take it for granted. They just grab what they want, but they don't think about their role as real leaders. What I think is when you're a good leader, really a good leader, you can feel it. Many of other people just think of themselves.*

These people turned our motto, which is "For God and my country," into "For God and my family" and "For god and my stomach." If our motto is "For God and my country," people elected as leaders, their purpose is to serve the people who trusted them with votes of power, but most of the time they just think of their families, their stomachs and what have you.

But in me, what I hear in me, really when people give me the opportunity to be their leader, I feel like I am like them, and I don't want to do anything that is not good. That is why I see that leadership is in the blood, and others have the blood that does not contain any leadership. It's a talent, it's a gift. And I have it. It is part of what it means to have a good life, to be a good man. I must also be *an easy man, a focused man, having a good relationship with everyone.*

I first realized I had the blood of leadership when I was Guild President in vocational school, but I now also use it in the Catholic Men's Group at church, and even in billiards. I am still very short, so many sports just aren't available to me, but I love to shoot pool, and I am quite good at it, and am well known, *a sort of celebrity.* I organize many kinds of tournaments. One I call the *"Candle Night Sniper." We switch off the electric lights, and then we put candles (that's the creativity I told you about) on the sides of the pockets of the pool table.* It's very popular.

We had one of those tournaments last night. It went very late. This morning, I am tired, and I will be late for work. As usual, my son Henry has helped me get ready. I went back into my bedroom to get some papers, and now I can't find him to say goodbye. He must be with his mom somewhere. I must go.

I quickly walk out our front door. My car is parked in our small, walled compound. Just outside the gate, I have improvised a cover for the very deep trench that runs along the road. This way, I can maneuver the car in and out of the space. I unlock the gate, then the car, and start it up. I put the car in reverse, and begin to back up when I realize that I have knocked into something. I pull forward again, and get out to assess the damage.

My God! It's my son! It's Henry!

How did this happen?

Why?

How did he get there?

I will ask myself these questions for years. Forever. *I tried to take him to the hospital, but he didn't survive.*

Luke

My name is Luke. I was born in 1959, and *I'm lucky. I was born in a hospital. During those days in 1959, not so many people were lucky to be born in a hospital. I was born at Mengo Hospital. It's a missionary hospital.*

I went to primary school, starting in 1966. I remember the year well because on my first day of school, the palace of the king was attacked. From our home, we looked down onto the area known as Mengo, where the palace is, and we could see so much smoke. While there is always some smoke rising from one of Kampala's seven hills--as farmers clear land with fire and as municipal workers burn rubbish--I had never seen smoke like this.

I also remember from day one, I never went to school barefooted. That was not common during those days. Almost the entire class had no shoes. (I remember one time they were looking for jiggers from all the students. I was the first to remove my shoes, but when I removed them, the class clapped because my feet were so clean.) I don't know how my mother managed, but she did her best for me.

I didn't know my father. I would ask my mom about him, but she never had much to tell me. But I liked school, and had many friends. They all asked me *about my father. I would tell them that my uncle was* actually *my father.* He was *the only man I really knew.*

When I was in *Primary 5,* Mum decided to take me into downtown Kampala. *We went to* buy *some clothes. I don't remember well whether it was Christmas or what, but we were in a shop,* and my *father happened to pass by! Mum saw him and called him. He came, we greeted each other, and she told me, "This is your father you've been asking for."*

My life changed that day. *I remember he paid for the clothes we had bought, and he went. Then I started pestering my mother to take me to my father. So one day, I think after our Primary 5 leaving examinations, the end of the year, she decided to take me there. I remember I slept there one night, then the next day Idi Amin took over power.* Even with the political revolution, I was able to carry on, so happy to now know my father.

After Primary 7, *I took the Primary Leaving Exams. I did them well and I passed. This led to my admission to secondary school, a very big school for the Brothers of Christian Instruction. So that's where I was admitted and I spent four years.*

During my first year, some of the students and staff planned a strike. *For us, we never knew that they were planning for a strike, we just learned when the strike* was *aborted. They had a plan to burn the whole school. Everything.* But *one of the students alerted the administration.*

Then we were all rounded up by police, the innocent and the planners of the strike. We were rounded up as criminals and we were taken to the police station where we spent the whole night. While I never had another problem like that at the school, I learned to be very cautious, to try to learn what others were planning, and I learned to distrust the police. How could they round us all up and detain us throughout the night!

Thankfully, I also learned to focus on my studies. My friends and I, though, well *we just hated science, so that prevented us from learning the subject. Mostly physics and mathematics.*

We were more interested in the arts where there are stories and the literature, where they had no calculations and what have you. But apart from that, I did all my A-level and I was admitted at another level.

Many other classmates were interested in having affairs with fellow students. For me, it was premature. It was not the time. We had to concentrate on studies. Others *were going for girls,* while those of us who did not *were seen as cursed, out of place, out of fashion.* We were not seen as cool kids.

But for me, I think that helped us to succeed. Because for instance, so many students *with whom I was in O-level, they are no more. They died. They died of AIDS. This means that, if I had also gone for sex, I would be no more. I mean during our time, it was not safe to be with the girls because of the deadly disease we are having. It took almost half of all my friends.*

The choice to abstain was so clear to me. But so many of my friends would say,

"We are not mahogany which will live for over seventy or eighty years. We have to enjoy life now."

Even up to now, we have people whom you tell, "Don't go," but still they go for many sexual partners. What's interesting is back then, during my schooling, *it was not like today. Then we had symptoms which could show you that that one is sick. So you could dodge them. But people we were blind. They were reckless.*

For me, I am a Pioneer member. In the Catholic Church, *we have a movement called the Pioneer Movement. The Pioneer Movement is purposely for self-control, abstaining from certain things for a given reason. We don't take alcohol. Not because alcohol is bad, but we don't take it as a prayer. We offer it because most people love alcohol. So for us, the thing which is loved the most is what we offer to God. It's good, we do like it, but we just offer it to God. I sacrifice for the people who abuse it, the drunkards. It eventually drives them to do wrong things. They cheat their partners. They deprive their homes of necessities because their money is channeled to the bottle. So for us, the reparation of the sins which are made by the drunkards, we offer the very good thing back to God. This helped us also to abstain from having early sexual intercourse which could lead to this anomaly.*

During my O Level, I was the Head-Boy, the leader of the students in my school. I learned a lot of things of how people behave, and this helped me to take care of my future. Because

when you go to A-level, your parents trust that
you are mature. They give you money for the
school fees and what have you, but I realized
that most of my colleagues were using that
money to give to girls to go gambling. So all
those anomalies, those short-comings, I learned
of them and I vowed to safeguard from them in
my future.

Later, *I went to teachers training college*
where I trained to become an educator, *and I*
was also a Guild Minister there. I tried to help
my colleagues. We tried to help each other. And
when I finished, I was posted to a deaf school
where I was a lay priest in charge of the bursary
for the school, and I helped train the teachers
there. *I worked there for several years.*

I even brought one of my family's boys there
to work and study when he failed to find school
fees. We used to call him Thursday, but he never
liked that name. So one day, they called me to the
family home in town where he was staying, and
we had a family meeting to assign him another
name.

I remember being excited about the meeting. I
decided to wear my paisley vest over a white shirt,
and my yellow tie with a smiley face on it. It says,
"Have a nice millennium!" It seemed fitting for
the occasion. When I arrived, I found everyone

enjoying their beers. They know that, for me, I don't take beers, so they gave me an orange soda, and we carried on until at last the Mama of the house decided to call him Mukasa Patrick. His life has not been so easy, but he has tried his level best. He tries seriously.

Back at the teachers training college, I did finally decide to get a girlfriend. *She was my colleague.* We spent time together, and learned about each other, but *then I realized I had no future with her.*

Fortunately, I got another one who is my present wife. But getting married here in our country is a challenge, maybe all over the world, but mostly here. You can be with more than one girlfriend, but *then to choose one becomes a problem because then that means the other will wage a war. Because it is natural. You have abandoned her and you have gone with another one. So I had the problem with the first one trying to discourage me to take the present wife that I am having, but I was focused and I said, "No way!" I had to stick to my decision.*

When you marry, there's another *problem here: the parents of the wife want their daughter to marry a well-to-do person so that you can support them also. Being a teacher, I had no money. So there were others who were discouraging* my wife *to move away from me, to divorce. But, I had the art of convincing her that better things are to come.*

This is what I call sadists. They are always *there to see one's downfall. They deny happiness. They would rather see you going through hard times. They want you to experience bad luck. They see you together with your wife, they don't want you to be together with your wife. They want you separated or divorced. So our people here are very funny. You never know what they like or what they hate, so it's only up to you to decide what is right and stick to it with God's guidance. But people were bent on breaking the marriage. God helped me and she never listened to them.*

It wasn't long before *we produced our first baby girl. When she had just given birth, I had a trip to Rome. I was a youth leader.* When I came *back, I passed where I had left her. The child was okay, and the mother and all the rest were okay. I told them, "Let me go to Masaka and report that I have come back," because it was the Masaka Diocese that had sent me. So I went.*

The following day, I saw my cousin-brother coming to see me, *very late in the night. I said, "What is it?"*

He said, "Your child is dead."

I said 'What?!! What has happened?'

He said, "They took the child to the hospital and she stayed there for an hour. She died."

I couldn't believe it, but when I came, it was so.

It was a sad experience. I lost my first born. We buried her. The whole extended family cried and grieved for two days.

~

Finally, *I decided to forget about the whole thing. Life had to continue.*

But *that was the period when AIDS was at its peak in Masaka. It started from Masaka.* And *my wife comes from Masaka. So when the child died,* people assumed it was because of HIV/AIDS. *I couldn't blame them for that because that was assumed all around. But we continued living. They only discovered that they were wrong after some time* when they saw that my wife and I, and our other kids, were not sick. *I only thank the Lord that he gave me the courage not to fight back. To get that courage to withstand the storm, really it was God's help.*

So, as I said, life had to continue.

We have had eight more children, including a set of twin boys. The oldest two have good jobs and are trying their best. The rest are still at home, and I have not yet been able to buy a house. We are renting, but we have some land that we tend. It is so important to me that my kids know how to dig and cultivate at least some of their own food. God has blessed us with a fruitful Uganda. We must utilize it.

And even me, I have more work to do before I die. In Uganda we say, "A man is not a man until he has a home." I have not yet built my own house. I must make sure I have that house built. Then I will truly be free to do what I want. I will finally be on my own.

That said, I am very respected in my community. People come to me for advice because I have lived life well. As an elected local government chairperson, *I have been rendering counseling services to parents who have children who are unruly. Caning can't solve much, but when you talk to a child and show him or her the future,* they can come to understand. *I have been engaged in this for the last seven or eight years, since I was first elected. We haven't had fresh elections because there's no money, so ever since that last election, I have been the chairperson.*

I have also *been helping people who divorce over little things. I sit with them. Even bigger people who are almost the age of my parents, they come to me. You know it is just a gift from God I think, because you come to me seeking advice and you are almost* the age of *my father?! Families which were threatened to fall apart are together again because of the counseling services I have been giving, telling them that "You are not alone. You are not the first to experience this." I am proud of that.*

I am also proud of *the upbringing of my children.* They are *healthy. That is the most important thing.* I have given *them proper medication,* and I have been *feeding them properly. I have educated them with my meager resources. There are people with money, but they have not educated their children. But for me, with meager resources I have improvised. I have God helping me, God on my side.*

And I have advised my children. I have given them a good example of how to work for a living. I have been engaged in practical farming. I have tried to clothe them. The girls have decent dresses. For the boys, I am avoiding torn trousers. Even if I buy old ones, they are decently dressed.

I have tried.

I have tried.

So, that gives me the confidence that really I have struggled, that I have neglected nothing.

Bennett

My name is Bennett, and I am 20 years old. *My mom gave birth to me at the age of 21, and it was quite a lovely life. We lived in a small house. As I continued growing, I went to school. It was fun.*

We used to carry plates in our bags so we could get lunch. The school provided the food, but we had to have our own plates. Everyone had the same style of plates: round plastic disks with a bowl-like indentation and a wide rim. They were very brightly colored in either blue, green, yellow or red. I think nearly every plate was either cracked or chipped, but we didn't get bothered. They still did the job. We didn't use cutlery, we used our fingers. Every day we had beans and posho made from cornmeal and water cooked to a dough-like consistency. We would mold the posho into a spoon-shape, use it to scoop up the beans, and then eat that spoon and make another one.

In my youngest years, I lived at my grandparents' house with my mum. When I was about four, Dad was finally able to rent a house, and *we started living together, but before that he was not around.*

Later on, my dad bought a car! I was really excited. It was fun. The night he brought it home, I raced out of the house, and jumped into the car. I sat tall in the driver's seat, and I had so much fun switching the headlights on-and-off. This model's lights raised up out of the front of the car when turned on, and then disappeared when off. "They remind me of eyelids," I told him. "Makes the car seem human." He laughed.

In Primary 2, my dad took me to boarding school. I stayed there up to Primary 6. The boarding session was quite good. I loved it, I got friends, it was lovely.

But then things started to change. My dad enrolled me in a different school, and I just didn't like it there. I don't know why he wanted me to leave my other school to come to this one.

At least *we used to have good lunch. We used to eat in* their *dishes. During the morning time, we would take porridge in some dish, and in the evening, they would wash them and use them for supper.*

I worked hard, and *I managed to get the first grade, and my dad was happy. He made me a promise: he was going to take me to shop because he knew I had passed well, but he came late. I saw him at the gate, but they did not allow him in. I cried.*

This is when my lovely life seemed to come apart. My parents started fighting. *In my life, I had never seen them quarrel, but I went home on a Sunday so that we could have lunch together. I heard these voices coming out of the bedroom. They were quarreling. I decided to leave as quickly as possible, and when I was leaving, my mom came out of the bedroom. I think she was crying. I had to say goodbye as quickly as possible, and I left.*

They separated shortly after that. And it wasn't long before Dad had a new wife. *She was a lady who disliked us. She used to cane us seriously,* and one time she *had boiled some water on the charcoal stove,* and she took my brother's hand and put it in that boiling water. I can still hear him screaming. But nothing happened to her. We just continued with our life.

The next day, *we had a sports day. That sports day was to be away from school because*

*our school had no soccer pitch. So we were told
to go, to move some kilometers out from the
school. As we were moving, we had to cross
Entebbe Road. As I was crossing, I was holding
my friend's hand. This boy took the first step
and was knocked down by a car. I myself, I
survived. I don't know how, but I survived. But I
was shocked and I fainted because the guy was
just near me, a zero distance.* And now *he was
dead.*

He had been such a good friend. He and I
were among the top three academic performers in
our school. And we often would pocket the
money our parents gave us for transportation,
and we would walk home together instead. We
would use the saved money to rent movies which
we would take turns watching in our own homes.
I had never actually been inside his house, and he
had never been in mine, but still we spent so
much time together.

He is also the one who first told me about
pornography. *I got so interested. I went to the
cyber cafe' and I searched about it. I was scared
and nervous at the first sight so I had to click it
off! I don't know how to call it, but it was new to
me. I was scared.*

I went back to school and prayed that my
lovely life would return to me. I mean I literally

prayed. A friend invited me to his church. It was very different than the Catholic masses I had attended with my grandmother. There was lots of singing and dancing, and the pastor seemed to more shout his sermon than speak it. He was telling us that Jesus was meant to be a personal Savior for each and every person. I sat there, and I don't know, I felt something funny in my body, like in my chest. The pastor kept talking and talking.

I looked around at the other people in the room. We were all seated on white plastic chairs. The church was still under construction. It had a roof and walls, but no glass in the windows, and no doors. But somehow it looked so beautiful to me. So different than when I had first entered.

"Stand up," the pastor said. "Stand up if you have made the decision to make Jesus your personal Lord and Savior."

"Should I?" I asked myself. "Should I try it?" I feel like I sat there for a long time debating myself, but I guess it couldn't have been too long, because I did find myself standing up with so many others. And I now feel much more at peace. I have gone to that church each and every Sunday since. And a bit of loveliness has come back.

I have started Secondary School in Kampala, and am doing well, though I am older than most of my classmates because for two years I sat at home due to a lack of school fees. I don't know if my dad is not working or what? He is gone a lot. He says he is traveling for work, but then when he returns, he says there is no money. At last, my Kojja Mukasa, the step-brother to my dad, has agreed to pay my fees, so at least I am studying again. He calls me "Big Boy Bennett" because he is too short.

In 2009, President Museveni announced that the Kabaka, the king of our tribe, would not be permitted to visit certain parts of his kingdom which is not fair, *so people started demonstrating. They started firing bullets and tear gas in the city. We were at school. Our teachers told us that we were going to end the lessons, and that we were going back home.*

You have to cross through the city to go back home, so the situation was hard. I had to gain my confidence, and I passed through the what? The city. I had to board a taxi right there from the middle of the city. There, the policemen, the army men were shooting, beating people, violating their rights.

As I was passing through, one policeman came near to me and told me, "Young boy, what are you doing in the city?" He said, "You are among the people who are demonstrating."

I told him, "No!"

But the man caught me, caught my hand, pulled me away, took me somewhere, started caning me seriously. I got some wounds on my ankle because the place on the body where he was caning me was the ankles, the elbows, and the back mainly.

Finally, he let me go, and I made my way back home. School resumed some days later.

I turned 20 six months ago and two days later, my elder sister gave birth to a baby boy. We were so happy. A month ago, I was at home for school holidays, together with this baby boy and my little sister when *a man came from nowhere. He's not a mad man, yet he came from nowhere, came into our home.*

I had given that baby to my little sister to carry for me as I was doing some work at home. So the man came and started fighting for the boy. He fought with the kid that I had given it to. He pulled and he fought. Accidently, they both let go of *the child, and the child landed on the ground.*

The baby didn't cry, the baby was alive. I was frightened.

I had nothing to do, I had to tell my sister. I told her, "Sister, this and this has happened."

We had to take the baby to the hospital, and he was examined. He was examined whereby he had a crack on the skull. The doctor told us to go to the police. We went to the police, we made a statement. The man was arrested and put inside.

After some days, about four, on my return to school as I had finished my exams, I called back at home to ask, "How is the baby?" I wanted to know how the baby was. On calling back home, they told me, "The baby has died."

This was two weeks back. And I had to board a boda boda and go back home and see what had happened. This man had been released! We tried to blame the man. The man wanted to fight my sister. The man fought me, he fought my brother, saying, "I had no problem, I had no problem with the case." He said it was the young girl who did it. So he denied it, so I had to leave the guy. But the guy is there, walking freely, and yet it is murder.

~

I don't understand so much of what is happening in my country. The president has signed a good new law that makes homosexuality very illegal, and yet people are still trying to recruit us to that behavior which *is condemned by most people. And I don't think it's good.*

But at least my Kojja Mukasa is helping me so that I can study. I was going to give up and just look for a job, but *I have friends who counseled me, who told me, "You know life is difficult in Uganda when you don't have papers." So I had to go back to school. I made up my mind. I read books. And now I take the best position in class.*

And for me, I am looking forward to making *a good life. I want to be a man of peace, a man who is not hated by many people, a man with no or few enemies, a man who is not worried.*

I will have unity in my family and my clan. I will see a better Uganda, a Uganda with no terrorism, no corruption, no tribalism; a country that is clean and one of the greatest in Africa.

I will be a grateful man who owns big businesses, travels long distances, a man who is supporting and caring, working to end the evil of street kids. To me, those are the ingredients of a good life.

And a good life I shall have.

Questions for Discussion and Reflection

Thursday/Patrick

1. What do you think the closed doors in young-Thursday's house are meant to symbolize?

2. Patrick continued to refuse to accept the former "housemaid" as his mother for four more years, and to this day he does not believe that one of his "uncles" is his father. Why do you think he struggles with this?

3. What role, if any, do you think Patrick's short stature plays in the way others assign him respect?

4. What does Patrick's reluctance to be honest with his uncle (about working more than studying) suggest about the dynamics between men and boys?

5.   Patrick's strong sense of independence--even deciding when he would return home and where he would sleep at age 15--is consistent with the study participants' sense of manhood. The fact that no one came looking for Patrick that night is meant to suggest that this feeling of independence is fostered by the other members of the community. The participants all felt entitled to this independence, and they felt great resentment when it was compromised either by employers, educators, the government, women or family. What implications does this have for those offering aid, for those working to alleviate poverty and address domestic violence, for example?

Luke

1.   Why did the author include the story about the shoes and the applause for the clean feet? Which larger constructs does this represent?

2.   What does the clash with police tell Luke about authority and the government's opinion of Luke and people like him?

3.   Discuss the absence of data suggesting nurturing care between male generations. What

implications does this have for understanding and serving this population?

4. "A man is not a man until he has a home." What does this mean? And why is practical farming so important?

5. What might motivate sadists in a setting like Uganda?

Bennett

1. Twice, Bennett discussed the food at school, and made a point of talking about using the school's plates instead of his own. Why do you think this is so important to him?

2. What do the events surrounding the death of Bennett's friend tell us about a life in poverty?

3. Again we see abuse from authority figures, both at home and in the street. How might this impact the development of a young man's world view?

4. Why do you think the participant talked about pornography in this discussion of "significant and important" life events?

5. By any assessment, Bennett's life has been extremely difficult, and yet his hopes for the future are clear and optimistic. What might be the reasons for this?

Further Discussion

This study investigated how masculinity is constructed for nine Ugandan male participants of three generations. The study explored their at-school lived experiences and their sense of engagement with and responsibility to other generations. This study was a qualitative investigation guided by a life history design. Narrative analysis was used to report the findings through the lens of adult development theory and within an ethical framework related to poverty.

Problem Statement

Although there has been a tremendous amount of research related to HIV, and to how women and children make meaning in the global

South [*sic*], little has been conducted about how men frame their own identities, or about how experiences with the formal education system and intergenerational relationships influence their notions of gender and personal wellness. This lack of understanding disempowers individuals and groups in efforts to effect personal and at-scale change.

Research Questions

The study's research questions are discussed below. The first two questions are connected, and are discussed as a whole.

How, if at all, did the at-school lived experiences of nine Ugandan men inform their notions of masculinity?

What are the notions of masculinity identified above, and how, if at all, have they evolved over three generations?

How, if at all, do nine Ugandan men express their sense of responsibility to provide nurturing care, in addition to financial support, to their children and families?

Discussion of Findings

At-School Lived Experiences

While efforts were made in the interviews to explore beyond the lived experiences of school-life and into the classrooms themselves, nothing of note emerged. Instead, the boarding school-life, the relationships it fosters (with fellow students) and the relationships it perhaps compromises (with family, for example) proved relevant.

Relationships, ranking, and reach. Initially, the participants were invited simply to plot "significant and important" life events on a timeline. For all of them, school played a prominent role on that line, highlighting the following informed notions of masculinity: the value of the aforementioned relationships, the importance of ranking amongst colleagues either in terms of academics or popularity--or both, and in the work of developing social and material capital via the education-escape from poverty.

Distrustful non-disclosure. The understandable construction of distrust is visible across the data--even beyond the school life--as the participants experienced abuse or loss at home, mistreatment by the police, attacks on their happiness by "sadists," and unfulfilled promises. This distrust appears to frequently lead to a hoarding of information, and a general tendency towards non-communication.

For example, as demonstrated, the men were even initially reluctant to participate in this study for these reasons. The 19 year old participant stated that he was hesitant to meet for the first interview because of the current public discourse that suggests that non-African men are visiting the country for the express purpose of "recruiting" young Ugandan men for same-sex engagement. "But when you talked about this project," he added, "my heart was fine. Then I was okay with whatever you were going to ask."

Once the participants were comfortable with the researcher's intentions and goals, the men became very eager to share their stories. Within the data, there is a strong indication that information is not normally shared, yet when trust was established (and perhaps because of the assurance of confidentiality), the hesitation was replaced by enthusiasm. It is very possible that they were making an effort to please the researcher, yet the depth of the conversations seemed to reveal otherwise, as did the findings of the focus group (in which the non-Ugandan investigator was not present).

There is another layer to this keenness. The idea that their lived experiences have value--to a stranger and to scholarship--appeared to be remarkably gratifying to them. This seems relevant to the guiding question about the reality of nurturing engagement between men. The participants' enthusiasm would suggest that perhaps they have been yearning for deeper connections than they had previously been afforded. This requires further investigation in order to be conclusive, but it begins to answer the third research question about intergenerational connectedness.

Responsibility and the Future

Here, the notion of resilience is compelling. These participants have not chosen simply to surrender. They have continued to pursue opportunities as they arrive, to improvise when necessary, and to maneuver around tremendous challenges. All of the characters and the participants might easily have abandoned the difficult quest for school fees in exchange for a simple job, or perhaps for a very basic life deep in their home village. Instead, they have chosen to remain in pursuit of a better life, and to share with the generation that follows. There seems to be a desire to thrive, a characteristic previously determined indicative of true resilience for humanity in general, and for Ugandan men specifically (Kizza, et al., 2012).

The Evil of Poverty

The findings repeatedly suggest the role of poverty in social construction. Every participant made multiple references to the frequent absence of school fees, for example, often costing them years of their life. Young men who value education for the reasons outlined above, but who struggled for the all important ranking simply because they either had been forced to skip entire levels of instruction, or because they had no time to study thanks to demanding work schedules.

Poverty also played a role via the weak infrastructure. The men spoke of dangerous roadways, the frequent power outages that made doing homework at night difficult if not impossible, and the challenge of accessing necessary supplies and books.

Many of these realities often led to a perfect storm of tragedy resulting in the death of friends, family, and children. The struggle to make sense of these realities while simultaneously working on self-awareness and self-advancement often seemed daunting if not impossible.

Plateaus of Adult Development

In assessing mental capacity, Kegan and Lahey (2009) look for moments when their study participants express times when they feel "angry, anxious/nervous, success, strong stand/conviction, sad torn, moved/touched, lost something/farewells, change, and important" (p. 22). These participants reflected at-length on all of these emotions.

In the eldest composite character's narrative, Luke's position as a counselor was included to demonstrate the eldest participants' appreciation for the respect they are given, but also their capacity to see into and understand the lives of others. When Luke says to his constituents, "You are not alone. You are not the first to experience this," he sounds very much like a person with a self-authoring mind. This is one of Kegan and Lahey's (2009) central descriptions of the plateau, the ability to "step back" and "evaluate" (p.17).

Conclusions

The notion that "we are not mahogany" emerges in each of the subcategories discussed above, either as a personal priority or as a way of life that the participants feel they must overcome.

When life is perceived as being very fragile and fleeting, the promise of survival does not exist, further fueling the desires and pleasures of the moment. This is its own plateau of development and thinking, a mindset that has an impact on one's identity as a man, and on the perceived legitimacy of a man's decisions.

Limitations of the Study

The Question of Generalizability

In the end, these are three stories as synthesized from only nine stories in the consideration of questions about how the many citizens of an entire culture construct notions of masculinity. While these findings may well be extremely unique, it is important to consider the notion of transferability (Lincoln & Guba, 1990) that suggests that knowledge from one setting will be useful in another setting if the two settings are similar. Whereas in the event that these finding truly are outliers, Donmoyer's (1990) psychological generalization notion values diversity and outliers, because diversity and outliers have the potential to expand our cognitive schema. In that latter argument, the potential diversity of these data could be treated as an insightful asset rather than an anomalous liability. That said, there is a possibility that this diversity was obscured in the process of creating three composite characters.

The Task of Tightening and Ordering

According to Polkinghorne (1995, p. 20), "The storied narrative form is not an imposition on data of an alien type but a tightening and ordering of experience by explicating an intrinsically meaningful form." The limitations then of this study are less about generalizability, and more about the process of "tightening and ordering of experience" (p. 20). In the quest to bring unity and meaning to the data, there is a risk of overreaching and over-interpreting within the creative-license and crafting of a good story that ultimately, because it is a composite of nine stories, most certainly is more of a fiction than a typical life history might normally be.

Implications for Further Research

This section describes several implications for further research. Additional qualitative interviews with a large number of male and/or female participants might further deepen the findings. An application of thematic analysis, followed by case studies and a cross-case analysis would likely add further layers of nuance and understanding.

Instrument Development

The development of an instrument would be useful to determine if these findings resonate with men at-scale, in other tribes and other East African nations. Ideally, the instrument could be administered via mobile technologies. A lesson learned in the early stages of this study is that the participants would likely need to be familiar with the principle investigator. Perhaps an existing database of men involved in other cohorts of research, or male clients of an educational or medical institution could be accessed.

Cohort Development

If no suitable telephone lists exist, then the creation of a cohort to engage with mobile-based research methods could prove very useful for this and other non-related investigations. Other cohorts could be populated by women, specific ethnic and age groups, and other demographically-specific subgroups.

Female Perspective

These findings could also be shared with women of the Buganda tribe, in matching age categories to look for resonance (or the lack thereof) in order to add deeper layers of understanding. Similarly, the women related to the men in this study could be invited to do their own timelines. The related timelines could then be mapped onto each other in a comparison of the separate and related constructions of femininity and masculinity.

Understanding Microlending Dynamics

According to Mpiira, et al. (2013), microlending is currently expanding in the region. Several models of microfinance build communities of shared responsibility and liability in which groups of individuals become responsible for each other's debts (Mpiira, et al., 2013). Research into this surprising intersection between distrust and cooperation could deepen understanding as well as inform practice through a model of how to scaffold projects that create trust where it otherwise does not seem to be.

Implications for Practice

The Work of Reflection

Participants in every age group expressed gratitude for this study's invitation to reflect. That fact, combined with the sense of satisfaction and pride they seemed to experience when they felt that their stories mattered, suggests that tools for reflection and the telling of stories could be incorporated into classroom instruction as well as into aid efforts and religious practices. By creating space for students, clients and parishioners to get to know themselves, while also sharing themselves with educators, aid workers and clergy, there is potential to effect deeper levels of change. In a sense, this might move the current models from a socialized approach to one that is more self-authoring, perhaps eventually leading to places that are actually transformative.

These reflections would likely need to have a creative approach as with this study's timeline and subsequent conversations. Other models might include expression through dance or drama, both are popular media in Uganda. The key appears to be in inviting voice and providing audience.

The Work of Capital

Although it is obvious, people's identity development will continue to be arrested unless issues of poverty are addressed. Too often, aid organizations work in isolation and not within the nested systems/ecosystems (Easterly, 2006). The apparently deep connection between material capital and social capital is not unique to Uganda, but it does seem pronounced in the context of abundant poverty. The work of eliminating or reducing poverty while simultaneously endeavoring to sever the connection between material and social capital would seem to be ideal, but very unlikely. Nevertheless, it is an implication of these findings.

The Work of Trust

These findings suggest that, in project or curriculum design, advanced work must be achieved to earn trust as well as to offer it. Without this baseline, interventions and offerings of care will continue to meet limited success instead of the elusive change-at-scale.

This trust might be established by identifying ways to privilege the sharing of information rather than the hoarding of it. By fostering and rewarding open communication, encouraging the opening of the metaphorical closed-doors, and by highlighting the value of transparency, students and clients might overcome the fear of sadism. The constant work of trying to surmise the intentions of others consumes cognitive space that could be focused on the deeper work of human flourishing.

Uganda

Uganda shares its borders with Kenya to the east, South Sudan to the north, the Democratic Republic of the Congo to the west, and Rwanda, Tanzania and Lake Victoria to the south. It is a former British colony and a current member of the British Commonwealth.

Recent Political History

From 1971 to 1979, Uganda suffered under the tyranny of President Idi Amin, an administration characterized by ethnic persecution and human rights abuses of the severest kind (Russell, 1999). In the years since, there has been significant economic progress, but there have also been the emergence and devastation of HIV/AIDS, numerous Ebola outbreaks, and a treacherous rebel war that stretched over many years and regions, affecting nearly every Ugandan life (Senyonyi, Ochieng, & Sells, 2012).

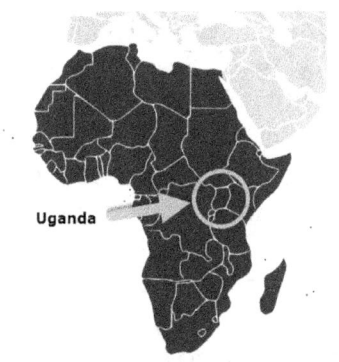

Currently, Uganda's President Yoweri Kaguta Museveni refuses to step down from the post he has held for 27 years, while rumors of a military coup dominate the headlines (Musa, 2013). This, combined with the fact that the misappropriation of foreign aid has reached an all-time high in the country, only further contributes to a general ethos of instability and uncertainty (Musa, 2013), an important factor to be sure in the consideration of meaning-making and masculinity. That is to say that as men make sense of their personal lives, it is, of course, within the larger context of their community. Given that Uganda's is a patriarchal society (Silberschmidt M. , 2001), the actions of the arguably most powerful man within the society are likely to influence personal perspectives as well.

In February of 2014, three Ugandan laws relevant to this discussion were signed into law. One makes it illegal for women to wear miniskirts because, according to the Ethics and Integrity Minister Simon Lokodo, they are worn for "the malicious purpose of exciting and stimulating" others (Heuler, 2014, p. 1). A second piece of legislation bans pornography and defines it as the "representation of the sexual parts of a person for primarily sexual excitement" (Bocast, 2014, p. 1). The third new law calls for life-imprisonment for anyone who engages in sexual activity with a person of their same gender, as well as punishment for anyone who offers advocacy or support for people who do so, and penalties for those who do not report such sexual behavior to police (Karimi & Thompson, 2014).

Education in Uganda

Uganda's education system is based on the British colonial model, and is made up of primary schools, grades 1-7, and secondary schools, grades S1-S4 and advanced levels 1 and 2 (UNESCO Institute for Statistics, 2011). In 2011, 79 percent of male children were enrolled in primary school, while 45 percent were enrolled in secondary school (UNESCO Institute for Statistics, 2011).

Since the late 1990's, health curriculum in both public and private schools has had a strong emphasis on HIV-prevention education (Education Abstract, 2011) and has been supplemented by a multi-sectoral approach to awareness including aggressive community counseling and expansive national media campaigns (Ministry of Health, 2014). Unlike many other African leaders, President Museveni was not reluctant to publicly discuss the formerly taboo topic of sexual activity, making HIV very much a part of the social and political discourse and landscape even now (Tumushabe, 2006).

Bibliography

Easterly, W. (2006). *The White Man's Burden: Why the West's Efforts to Aid the Rest Have Done So Much Ill and So Little Good.* New York: Penguin.

Lincoln, Y., & Guba, E. (1990). Judging the Quality of Case Study Reports. *International Journal of Qualitative Studies in Education, 3* (1), 53-59.

Mpiira, S., Kiiza, B., Katungi, E., Staver, C., Tabuti, J., Kiyotalimye, M., et al. (2013). Factors influencing households participation in the Savings and Credit Cooperative (SACCO) programmes in Uganda. *African Journal of Agricultural Research, 8* (43), 5280-5288.

Acknowledgements

I wish to thank my Ugandan colleagues for their insights which made this project possible, and for their patience with me as I pursued it. Dean Paula Cordeiro truly is the finest mentor, chair and friend I could have possibly asked for in this process. I feel unimaginably blessed. To my committee members, I still can't believe you said yes! This work is also yours. To Rod and Diane Dammeyer, I simply would not have been able to do this without your support. I will forever feel honored to have been the first Dammeyer Fellow, and I shall work very hard to multiply your investment. To Catherine Reynolds, if I had not been a Reynolds Fellow at Harvard University, neither would I have succeeded here. To Professor Howard Gardner for your important input on this study.

To my colleagues who have supported me in so many brilliant and practical ways along the way: Emily Rapley, Commander Melanie Hitchcock, Dr. Tricia Rhodes, Dr. Leslie Hennessey, Dr. Rachel Rice, and Maureen

Guarcello. To by colleagues in the SOLES Global Center, Dean Linda Dews, Mara Vicente Robinson, Peter Maribei, Kedir Assefa Tessema, and Corrine Brion, you filled the journey with light and laughter.

To AidChild's board of directors and board of advisors, thank you for giving me the space and support that I needed for this work. To AidChild's donors, partners and friends, I felt your prayers and cheers on many occasions along the way.

To Austin Unterbrink, for helping me pursue physical wellness as I built mental muscle. To Nsereko Tom and Jjumba Henry for being uncles to my kids while Dad was gone. To Monica Millard for being a generous host and a great sounding board as I collected my data.

To my sweet sister, Hannah, who started calling me doctor long before I earned the title (glad you didn't jinx it!). And to my dearest parents who see none of my flaws, exaggerate my strengths, and who gave me a rock solid education by homeschooling me. Onward.

About the Author

Dr. Dunigan is the founder of AidChild, the first organization to offer free antiretroviral medication to children living with AIDS in Uganda. He lived in the village of Masaka for nine years before pursuing his academic career. He holds a PhD in Leadership Studies from the University of San Diego where he was the Dammeyer Fellow in Global Education Leadership. He also holds a Master's Degree in Human Development and Psychology from Harvard University where he was a Reynolds Fellow in Social Entrepreneurship, and winner of the 2010 Harvard HDP Marshal Award. Prior to his move to Uganda in 2000, Nathaniel was Deputy Director of the Office of the Governor of Arizona, and Director of Education at Leadership Ministries.

Please visit the following to learn more:
www.aidchild.org
www.NathanielDunigan.com
www.DrDunigan.com